Prayers from the Heart
for the Feasts of the Year

for Philip Trower with love and thanks

Prayers from the Heart for the Feasts of the Year

Joanna Bogle

First Published 1992

Gracewing

Fowler Wright Books
Southern Avenue
Leominster
Herefordshire HR6 0QF

Gracewing Books are distributed

In New Zealand by
Catholic Supplies Ltd
80 Adelaide Rd
Wellington
New Zealand

In Australia by
Charles Paine Pty
8 Ferris Street
North Parramatta
NSW 2151 Australia

In Canada by
Novalis
PO Box 990
Outremont H2V 457
Canada

In USA by
Morehouse Publishing
P.O. Box 1321
Harrisburg
PA 17105
U.S.A.

Cover design & interior illustrations by Gill Onions

ISBN 0 85244 202 5

Typesetting by Print Origination (NW) Ltd., Formby, Liverpool L37 8EG
Printed and bound by Billings & Sons Ltd Worcester

Introduction

A little while ago, I produced 'A Book of Feasts and Seasons', giving ideas on how to celebrate all the traditional feasts of the Christian year at home. It was lovely finding out about all the the different ways of honouring the various festivals that take place – scarcely a week goes by without something important and valuable coming up in the calendar, and there is a wealth of recipes, games, and rituals to discover.

But of course the main reason for the annual cycle of the various feasts is prayer. We may not always be able to gather together to mark a special day with family or friends, but we can always honour it in prayer. And down the centuries Christians have always done this, and produced prayers for every possible occasion.

These prayers can be used either by families praying together, or by people alone – in church, at home, or in some quiet corner. There are prayers not only for the great feasts such as Christmas and Easter, with their preparatory seasons of Advent and Lent, but for many of the saint's days and other minor feasts: the Annunciation ('Lady Day'), St Francis, St George, St Lucy, Our Lady's Birthday, All Saints and All souls.

Life need never be dull for a Christian – the annual round of the seasons is always giving us something new to discover, and to think about. And when we celebrate here on earth, we can know that they are celebrating in Heaven, too!

Joanna Bogle

Acknowledgements

The following Bible extracts are from the Authorised Version of the Bible, the copyright of which is vested in the Crown and are reprinted with permission of the Crown's patentee, Cambridge University Press: Matthew 2:2, Luke 1:46–55; Joel 2:12–13; Isiah 66:10,11; Matthew 5:3–12; Psalm 130. The Funeral Service prayer is from the Book of Common Prayer of 1662. The rights of this are vested in the Crown in perpetuity within the United Kingdom, and the prayer is reproduced by permission of the Crown's patentee, Cambridge University Press. The prayer for Hanukkah comes from 'Praying with the Jewish Tradition' Edizione Paoline SRL, Milan. Efforts have been made to trace the copyright of all the prayers used. Dunstan Thompson's poem 'San Salvador' is reprinted from his 'Poems 1950–1974' with permission from Philip Trower. The prayer to Our Lady of England is published with permission from the White Canons of Premontre at the Shrine of Our Lady of England, Storrington, Sussex. The prayers for Advent and Pentecost by the four Lithuanian girls are reprinted with the permission of Aid to the Church in Need and the prayers of Cardinal Wyszinski with permission of Harcourt Brace Janovich Inc and Editions de Dialogu Paris. The Lithuanian girls' prayers appear in 'Mary Save Us', distributed by Aid to the Church in Need, and Cardinal Wyszinski's prayers in 'A Freedom Within' also distributed by Aid to the Church in Need. I thank Mrs. Veronica Pierson for introducing me to the prayer used in the commissioning of HMS Vindex with her father captain 'Bill' Bayliss in command.

PRAYERS FOR THE NEW YEAR AND SPRING FEASTS

New Year

God has created me to do Him some definite service. He has committed some work to me which He has not committed to another. I have my mission. I may never know it in this life, but I shall be told it in the next. I am a link in a chain, a band of connection between persons. He has not created me for naught. I shall do good, I shall do His work. I shall be an angel of peace, a preacher of truth in my own place, while intending it – if I do but keep His Commandment – therefore I will trust Him. Whatever, where I am I can never be thown away. If I am in sickness my sickness may serve Him, in perplexity, my perplexity may serve Him; if I am in sorrow, my sorrow may serve Him. He does nothing in vain, He knows what He is about. He may take away my friends, He may throw me among strangers. He may make me feel desolate, make my spirits sink, hide my future from me – still He knows what He is about.

John Henry Newman 1801–90

New Year

O God, the sea is so wide, and my boat is so small
Be good to me.

Breton fisherman's prayer

I said to the man who stood at the Gate of the Year:
"Give me a light that I may tread safely into the
unknown". And he replied "Go out into the
darkness and put your hand into the hand of God.
That shall be to you better and safer than a known
way."

Minnie Haskyns 1875–1957

What doth the Lord require of thee
but to do justly, and
to love mercy,
and to walk humbly with thy God?

Micah: 6:8

New Year

''*What do ye fear, seeing that God the Father is
     with you?*''
''*We fear nothing*''
''*What do ye fear, seeing that God the Son is with
     you?*''
''*We fear nothing*''
''*What do ye fear, seeing that God the Holy Spirit
     is with you?*''
''*We fear nothing*''

*May the Almighty God, for the sake of His Son
Jesus Christ, through the comfort of the Holy
Ghost, the one God who brought the Apostle Paul,
with his ship, and the crew, out of the great tempest
and out of the fierce storm, save us, and sanctify us,
and carry us on in favouring winds, and comfort, over
the sea and into harbour according to His own good
will, which things we do for Him'.*

*Dedication service at the commisssioning of HMS Vindex, 1943.
Captain 'Bill' Bayliss in command.*

Epiphany – January 6th

The word 'Epiphany' comes from the Greek, and means a manifestation or appearance – in this case the appearance of Christ as God to the gentiles, in the persons of the Magi, and to others at His baptism in the Jordan, and His first miracle at Cana.

Manifest at Jordan's stream
Prophet, Priest and King supreme;
And at the Cana wedding-guest
In Thy Godhead manifest;
Manifest in power divine,
Changing water into wine;
Anthems be to Thee addrest,
God in Man made manifest.

Christopher Wordsworth 1807–1885

Epiphany – January 6th

O God, who on this day didst manifest Thine only-begotten Son to the Gentiles by the guidance of a star; graciously grant that we, who know Thee now by faith, may be led even to contemplate the beauty of Thy Majesty.

Old Collect for Epiphany

We have seen His star in the East, and are come with gifts to adore the Lord.

Matthew 2:2

Candlemas – February 2nd

Candlemas is the ancient feast marking the Presentation of Christ as a baby in the Temple. On that occasion, Simeon said Christ was 'A light to lighten the Gentiles', but warned Mary 'A sword will pierce your heart also'. We light candles at ceremonies in churches on this day to commemorate his words and to honour Christ as the Light of the World. Candlemas also marks the final end of the Christmas season: long ago this was the day when people took down their Christmas decorations.

O Mary, pierced with sorrow
Remember, reach and save
The Soul that goes tomorrow
Before the God that gave;
As each was born of woman
For each, in utter need
True comrade and brave foeman
Madonna, intercede.

Rudyard Kipling 1886–1936

This comes from his poem 'God of Battles', a prayer for soldiers to say before going to war.

St. David, Patron Saint of Wales – March 1st

St David (died 601 AD), was a monk and Bishop of the 6th century. Not only was he the only Welsh saint to be canonized in the Western church, but he may have founded as many as 10 monasteries where the monks lived in extreme austerity. His name was often spelled 'Dafydd' from which comes 'Taffy' – the colloquial name for Welshmen.

Am iechyd da a bwyd bob pryd
Molinnwn di O Dduw.

For good health and every meal
We praise thee O God.

An old Grace before Meals (Welsh)

St. Patrick's Day – March 17th

Christ with me, Christ before me, Christ behind me,
Christ within me, Christ beneath me, Christ above
*   me,*
Christ at my right hand, Christ at my left,
Christ in the fortress, Christ driving the chariot,
*   Christ steering the ship,*
Christ in the heart of every man who thinks of me,
Christ on the lips of every man that speaks to me,
Christ in every eye that sees me,
Christ in every ear that hears me.

Ascribed to St Patrick c.390–c.460

St. Joseph – March 19th

Chosen thou wert by thy Maker's decree
Spotless virginity's bridegroom to be
Thee the Eternal his father would call
Steward on earth of his bounty to all.

Glory to God, Three in One, let us own
Who 'mid the angels thy merits doth crown
Would but He grant, through those merits that we
Live everlastingly, Joseph, with thee.

17th cent. tr. Ronald Knox

Annunciation – March 25th

My soul doth magnify the Lord,
my spirit hath rejoiced in God, my Saviour.
For He hath regarded the low estate of His
handmaiden: for behold
from henceforth all generations shall call me blessed.
For He that is mighty hath done to me great things;
and Holy is His name. And
His mercy is on them that fear Him from
generation to generation.
He hath shewed the strength of His arm; He hath
scattered the proud in the imagination of their hearts.
He hath put down the mighty from their seats
and exalted them of low degree.
He hath filled the hungry with good things,
and the rich He hath sent empty away.
He hath holpen His servant, Israel, in
remembrance of His mercy;
As He spake to our fathers, to Abraham and to his
seed for ever.

Magnificat (Luke 1:46–55)

Annunciation – March 25th

O full of grace, all creation, the angelic host and the race of men, rejoices in you; holy sanctuary, spiritual paradise, glory of virgins from whom God took flesh; He was God before all the time became a little Child within you. Your lap was His throne, and your womb He made greater than the sky. All creatures are joyful in you, O full of grace. Glory to you.

Hymn of Praise for the Byzantine Liturgy of St. Basil

All Fools Day – April 1st

Give us good cheer this day, O Lord: show us how to enjoy good humour! Thank you for your gift of laughter – may we use it as you would wish.

cc. J. Bogle 1991

PRAYERS FOR LENT

Ash Wednesday – the first day of Lent

On this day, ashes are traditionally blessed and distributed to churches; the priest makes a tiny Sign of the Cross on the forehead of each person, saying "Repent, and believe in the Gospel"

Almighty and everlasting God . . . spare the penitent . . . bless these ashes, that they may be a remedy to all who invoke Thy name . . . O God, who desires not the death but the conversion of sinners, look in kindness upon our human frailty . . . so that we, who know ourselves to be but ashes, and that we must return to dust, may deserve to obtain pardon, and the rewards offered to the penitent.

Traditional meditation for Ash Wednesday

Ash Wednesday – the first day of Lent

My God, accept my heart this day
And make it wholly Thine
That I from Thee no more may stray
No more from Thee decline

Matthew Bridges 1800–1894

'Therefore also now, saith the Lord, turn ye even to me with all your heart, and with fasting, and with weeping, and with mourning. And rend your heart, and not your garments and turn unto the Lord your God: for he is gracious and merciful, slow to anger, and of great kindness, and repenteth him of evil.'

Joel 2:12–13

Lent

O Lord our God
grant us grace to desire Thee with our whole heart;
that, so desiring, we may seek,
and, seeking, find Thee;
and so finding Thee, may love Thee;
and loving Thee, may hate those sins
from which Thou hast redeemed us.

St. Anselm (died 1109)

They alone are able truly to enjoy this world, who
begin with the world unseen. They alone enjoy it,
who have first abstained from it. They alone can
truly feast, who have first fasted; they alone are able
to use the world, who have learned not to abuse it;
they alone inherit it, who take it as a shadow of the
world to come, and who for that world to come
relinquish it.

John Henry Newman 1801–90

Lent

I love you, Jesus, my love above all things; I repent with my whole heart of having offended you. Never allow me to separate myself from you again. Grant that I may love you always and then do with me what you will.

Traditional Lenten prayer

Lord Jesus my Saviour, let me now come to Thee:
My heart is cold; O Lord warm it by Thy selfless love.
My heart is sinful; cleanse it by Thy precious blood.
My heart is weak; strengthen it by Thy Joyous Spirit.
My heart is empty; fill it with Thy Divine Presence.
Lord Jesus my heart is Thine; possess it always and only for Thyself. Amen.

St. Augustine of Hippo 354–430 AD

Lent

I saw the Son of God go by
Crowned with a crown of thorn.
"Was it not finished, Lord?" said I
"And all the anguish borne?"
He turned on me His awful eyes:
"Hast thou not understood?
Lo, every soul is Calvary
and every sin a rood."*

Rachel Anard Taylor, 'The Question', from Anthology of Jesus, edited by Sir James Marchant.

*rood, meaning 'wood' is the old English word for the Cross.

O Lord Jesus Christ, who didst create me, redeem me, and foreordain me for that which I now am; Thou knowest what Thou wilt do with me: deal with me according to Thy most compassionate will. I know and confess in sincerity that in Thy hand all things are set, and there is none that can withstand Thee. Thou art Lord of all.

King Henry VI, d.1471

Lent

Friend of the friendless, and the One who cares
For every lonely, frightened, desperate man;
Kind Heart, attentive to the feeblest prayers,
Hastening to all who do the best they can;
Dear Host, sole owner of the house He built,
Who, coming unexpected to the door,
Knocks, and, if answered, breaks the chain of guilt,
And lets the soul go free to live once more;
Shepherd, who seeks His torn and filthy sheep,
Rejoicing when the longest lost is found;
Father, who sees the broken wastrel creep
Towards home, and running, lifts him from the
ground;
This is our God, entreating us to prove
His friends and live forever in His love.

Dunstan Thompson 1918–1975, 'San Salvador'

Mothering Sunday – (fourth Sunday in Lent)

Don't let anyone tell you that Mothering Sunday began in the 18th century when servant-girls went home for the day to visit their mothers! It is far, far older that that. We have to ask why they went home on this praticular day. It was because it had already been done for centuries. The fourth Sunday in Lent is Laetare Sunday, the day on which the Church invites everyone to take a break from the fasting and remember that Easter is on the way (the Latin word laetare means 'rejoice'). Earlier, in pagan times, people had honoured the goddess of motherhood at this time of the year on the feast of Matronalia. So the Church made Laetare Sunday a day when people honoured Mother Church. They went home to their own home parishes if they happened to be far away on that day. And the traditional food is simnel cake, from similia, the cakes of fine white flour that the ancient pagan Romans used on Matronalia.

Rejoice ye with Jerusalem: and be glad with her, all ye that love her: rejoice for joy with her, all ye that mourn for her: that ye may suck, and be satisfied with the breasts of her consolations.

Isaiah 66:10, 11; the Introit for Laetare Sunday

PRAYERS FOR HOLY WEEK AND EASTER

Palm Sunday

All glory, laud and honour
To Thee, Redeemer, King!
To whom the lips of children
Made sweet hosannas ring.
Thou art the King of Israel
Thou David's royal Son
Who in the Lord's name cometh
The King and Blessed One.

The people of the Hebrews
With palms before Thee went
Our praise and prayers and anthems
Before Thee we present.

To Thee before Thy Passion
They sang their hymns of praise
To Thee, now high exalted
Our melody we raise

Thou didst accept their praises
Accept the prayers we bring
Who in all good delighteth
Thou good and gracious King.

St. Theodulph, Bishop of Orleans, written at Anjou 820 AD

Holy Week

We adore Thee, O Christ, and we praise Thee
Because by Thy Holy Cross Thou hast redeemed
the world

Traditional prayer

Lord Jesus Christ, have mercy on me, a sinner.

The Jesus Prayer, 6th century

Popularised as the prayer of a Russian pilgrim in search of God

Good Friday

Hail, most sweet Jesus, whose heart was opened by a soldier's spear. Of Thy mercy, take from me my forward heart, and give me a loving and faithful one like unto Thine.

Ancient Carthusian Prayer

Thanks be to Thee, my Lord Jesus Christ for all the benefits Thou hast won for me, For all the pains and insults Thou hast borne for me.

O most merciful Redeemer, Friend, and Brother, may I know Thee more clearly, love Thee more dearly and follow Thee more nearly for ever and ever. Amen.

St. Richard of Chichester c. 1197–1253

Good Friday

My good and dear Jesus
I kneel before you
asking you most earnestly
to engrave upon my heart
a deep and lively faith, hope, and charity,
with a true repentence, for my sins
and a firm resolve to make amends.
As I reflect upon your five wounds,
and dwell upon them with deep compassion and grief,
I recall, good Jesus, the words the prophet David
spoke long ago concerning You:
'They have pierced my hands and feet,
they have counted all my bones'.

Traditional

Good Friday

He mine by gift – I His by debt

Robert Southwell 1561–1595
Found scratched on the wall of his death-cell in the Tower of London,
where he was imprisoned for his faith

Rock of ages, cleft for me
Let me hide myself in Thee
Let the water and the blood
From Thy side a healing flood
Be of sin the double cure
Save from wrath, and make me pure.

Augustus Toplady 1740–1778

Easter Sunday

When the stone had been sealed by the Jews, and when the soldiers were watching Thy Sacred Body, Thou, O Saviour, didst arise on the third day and give Life to the World. Wherefore the Powers of Heaven cry to Thee, O Giver of Life: Glory to Thy Resurrection, O Christ; glory to Thy Kingdom; glory to Thy dispensation, O Thou Who alone art Merciful.

From the Divine Liturgy of St. John Chrysostom

O world invisible, we view thee
O world intangible, we touch thee
O world unknowable, we know thee
In apprehensible, we clutch thee!

Francis Thompson 1859–1907

Ascension Day

The Ascension of Our Lord – the open gates of Heaven allow all wanderers to gaze at the heavens with the insight of faith, with the eyes of hope. When Heaven is open, one's entire life seems to be but a tear rolling down the face of the newborn. The Sun of Life will soon dry it and embrace it with the rays of its fervent love. And love is without end.

Cleanse me, then, as You cleansed the Samaritan woman, Mary Magdalene, the public sinner. Give me Your Hand, as You gave it to Peter on the waves of the sea. Open my eyes, as You opened them for the blind man of Jericho and the man blind from birth. Lead me from the grave, as You led Lazarus. Let me touch Your side, as You let Thomas touch it. Increase my faith and teach me to pray, as You taught the Apostles. And give me love, as You did to Mary, so that I may love much. Love is, after all, the greatest virtue of Heaven's inhabitants.

Cardinal Stephen Wyszinski, former primate of Poland, d. 1983.

This prayer was written on Ascension Day 1955, when he was in prison under the Communist regime.

Ascension Day

Grant, Lord, that our longing may follow Thee
there,
On earth who are thronging thy temples with prayer;
And unto Thee gather, Redemmer, thine own
Where Thou with Thy Father dost sit on the throne.

The Venerable Bede 673–735
tr. Ronald Knox 1888–1957

PRAYERS FOR TRINITY AND AFTER

Trinity Sunday – 1st Sunday after Pentecost

Holy, holy, holy! Lord God Almighty
early in the morning our song shall rise to Thee
Holy, holy, holy! merciful and mighty
God in three persons, blessed Trinity.

Holy, holy, holy! all the saints adore Thee
Casting down their golden crowns around the glassy
sea
Cherubim and seraphim falling before Thee
God everlasting through eternity.

Reginald Heber 1783–1826

Trinity Sunday

Praise God, from whom all blessings flow
Praise Him, all creatures here belolw
Praise Him above, ye heavenly host;
Praise Father, Son, and Holy Ghost.

Thomas Ken 1637–1711

Trinity Sunday

O Holy God, holy and mighty, holy immortal, have mercy upon us. (thrice)

Glory be to the Father, and to the Son, and to the Holy Ghost,

Both now and for ever and world without end. Amen.

Most holy Trinity, have mercy upon us.

O Lord, purge our sins.

O Master, pardon our iniquities.

O Holy One, visit and heal infirmities, for Thy Name's sake.

Lord, have mercy upon us. (thrice)

Glory be to the Father, and to the Son, and to the Holy Ghost.

Both now, and for ever and world without end. Amen.

The 'Thrice-holy Hymn' atrib. to St. John Chrysostom c.347–407

Trinity Sunday

Firmly I believe and truly
God is Three and God is One;
And I next acknowledge duly
Manhood taken by the Son.

And I trust and hope most fully
In that Manhood crucified
And each thought and deed unruly
Do to death, as He has died.
Simply to His grace and wholly
Light and life strength belong
And I love supremely, solely,
Him the holy, Him the strong.

And I hold in veneration
For the love of Him alone
Holy Church, as His creation
And her teachings as His own.

Adoration aye be given
With and through the angelic host
To the God of earth and Heaven
Father, Son, and Holy Ghost.

John Henry Newman 1801–90

Pentecost

Breathe in me, Holy Spirit,
that I may think what is holy
Move me, Holy Spirit, that I may do what is holy,
Attract me, Holy Spirit,
that I may love what is holy,
Strengthen me, Holy Spirit,
that I may guard what is holy,
Guard me, Holy Spirit,
that I may keep what is holy.

St. Augustine of Hippo AD 354–430

Come, O Holy Spirit, fill the hearts of Thy faithful
and kindle in them the fire of Thy love.
Send forth Thy spirit and they shall be created,
and Thou shalt renew the face of the earth.

Traditional

Pentecost

Waiting for the promised Paraclete
the apostles prayed ardently
together with Jesus' Mother.

Then the day of Pentecost came
and flames of fire
descended upon them,
enlightening them
and bringing them
apostolic fervour,
the courage of the martyrs,
wisdom,
and the gift of tongues.

Come, Holy Spirit,
Comforter and Confirmer,
come down on us.
We are waiting for You;
We are asking for You;
We are praying for You.

Pentecost

Come and renew us
Come and revive our nation.

Bring us all the graces we need
that, united by love
we may establish
God's kingdom
in our homeland. Amen

This prayer was written by four Lithuanian girls deported to Siberia in 1953. It is one of several prayers in a hand-written prayer book which they stitched together: it measured 2 inches by 3 inches and they managed to get it back to a friend in Lithuania, from where it later found its way abroad, to be published in eight languages.

Pentecost

Breathe on me, breath if God
Fill me with life anew
That I may love what thou dost love
And do what thou wouldst do.

Edwin Hatch 1853–1889

Midsummer Day – June 24th

For the beauty of the earth,
for the beauty of the skies,
for the love which from our birth
over and around us lies

For each perfect gift of thine
to our race so freely given
graces human and divine
flowers of each and buds of Heaven

Christ our God, to thee we raise
this our scrifice of praise.

Folliott Sandford Pierpoint 1835–1917

St. Peter and St. Paul – June 29th

Before the cock crew twice –
dread hour of trial –
the Apostle uttered thrice
his dark denial.

And then the Saviour turned,
on Peter gazing –
a look divine, that yearned
with love amazing.

Swiftly to Peter's face
the shame came leaping:
he had denied such grace,
and went forth weeping.

Lord Jesus, look on me,
your kind face turning;
my soul with agony
of sin is burning.

The way is long, I find
my weak steps falling
O turn, to my dark mind
your grace recalling.

Hallgrim Pjetursson 1614–174
tr. Charles Venn Picher 1879–1961

Mary's Assumption – August 15th

O Christ, before whose throne of grace
Thy mother stands to plead our case,
Exert thy love, and grant that we
May share Thy Father's clemency

Ascribed to Rabanus Marcus 776–856

May today's venerable festivity, O Lord, bring us
salutory aid, whereon God's Holy Mother
underwent temporal death, yet could not be held
down by the shackles of death, she who bore Your
Son made flesh of her.

Gregorian Sacramentary, Sixth Century

Mary's Assumption – August 15th

There are three things that render death bitter: attachment to the world, remorse for sins, and the uncertainty of salvation. The death of Mary was entirely free from these causes of bitterness, and was accompanied by three special graces, which rendered it precious and full of joy. She died as she had lived, entirely detached from the things of the world; she died in the most perfect peace; she died in the certainty of eternal glory.

St. Alphonsus Ligouri d. 1787

PRAYERS FOR THE HARVEST

Harvest

Bless these Thy gifts, most gracious God,
From whom all goodness springs;
Make clean our hearts and feed our souls
With good and joyful things.

An old Grace before meals.

For seasonable weather, for the abundance of the
fruits of the earth and for peaceful times, let us
beseech the Lord. Lord, have mercy.

From the Divine Liturgy of St. John Chrysostom

Harvest

We plough the fields and scatter
the good seed on the land
But it is fed and watered by God's Almighty hand
He sends the snow in winter,
the warmth to swell the grain
The breezes and the sunshine,
and soft refreshing rain
All good things around us are sent from
Heaven above
Then thank the Lord, O thank the Lord,
for all His love

We thank Thee then O Father,
for all things bright and good
The seed-time and the harvest,
our life, our health, our food,
Accept the gifts we offer, for all Thy love imparts
And, what Thou most desires,
our humble, thankful hearts.

Matthias Claudias 1740–1815

Harvest

The Lord is good to me and so I thank the Lord
For giving me the things I need;
The sun, the rain, and the appleseed.
The Lord is good to me.

Johnny Appleseed 1774–1845
American pioneer who planted apple orchards in Pennsylvania.

O Lord, the merciful and good,
Bless and sanctify our food.
Grant they to us may wholesome be,
And make us thankful unto thee.

Anon 1671

Father of Mercies, by whose love abounding
All we thy Creatures are sustained and fed;
May we while here on Earth thy praises sounding
Up to they Heavenly Courts in joy be led.

Grace used by the children of the Foundation Hospital in London's
Guildford Street, founded 1739 and running until 1926.

Laudi Spirituali

For these and all thy mercies given,
We bless and praise thy name, O Lord!
May we receive them with thanksgiving,
Ever trusting in thy word.
To thee alone be honour, glory,
Now and hence forth for evermore
Amen

Sung as a Grace by many London Livery Companies, 1545

Birthday of the Virgin Mary
– September 8th

'To be the Mother of God is a prerogative so lofty,
so tremendous as to surpass all understanding. There
is no honour, no beatitude capable of approaching
an elevation which consists in being, of the whole
human race the sole person superior to all others,
unequalled in the prerogative of having one common
Son with the Heavenly Father.'

Martin Luther 1483–1546

Birthday of the Virgin Mary
– September 8th

Your Nativity, O Virgin Mother of God, has proclaimed joy throughout the whole world, for from you the Sun of Righteousness, Christ our God, has shone, Who has destroyed the curse and given blessings, laid death aside and gave us eternal life.

Prayer from Old Slavonic Byzantine Rite for the Birthday of the Virgin Mary.

In Medieval times, The Birthday of the Virgin Mary was celebrated as a holiday. Devotion to Mary was widespread, and flowers and even insects bear her name, such as marigolds, and ladybirds.

Prayer to our Lady of England

O Glorious and Blessed Mary, our Mother and our Queen, we gladly acclaim you as our 'Lady of England'.

We thank you for all the graces which you have obtained for this country in times past and ask you to obtain still more.

Grant that, as this nation of ours once worshipped God through one Church, so by your intercession, may all Christians be reunited in the one service of your Son, and may all our fellow countrymen come to the knowledge and love of this same Son,

Our Lord Jesus Christ.

Our Lady of England, pray for us.

Our Lady of England, bless our country.

Our Lady of England, unite all Christians into one Church.

Our Lady of England Priory, Storrington, Sussex

Michaelmas – September 29th

Holy Michael, Archangel
Defend us in the day of battle.
Be thou our safeguard against the wickedness
and snares of the devil.
May God rebuke him, we humbly pray,
and do thou, Prince of the Heavenly Host, thrust
down into Hell Satan and all wicked spirits
Who wander through the world for the ruin of souls.
Amen.

Traditional

Michaelmas – September 29th

The splendour of the Father's rays
Thee, our heart's life, we gladly praise,
Jesus, our hymns to Thee we bring
And 'midst Thy prostrate angels sing.

Ten thousand warriors armed on high
Embattled angels fill the sky.
Michael the conquering chief appears,
On high the glorious Cross he rears.

He with salvation's sign unfurled
The dragon down the abyss has hurled
The rebels with their chief are driven
Scathed by the lightning flash, from Heaven.

Then faithful at the chieftain's side
Pursue the hateful king of pride
Till from the Lamb a heavenly crown
Rewards us with unquenched renown.

Ascribed to Rabanus Mairus, 776–856

Guardian Angels – October 2nd

They come, God's messengers of love,
They come from realms of peace above,
From homes of never-fading light,
From blissful mansions ever bright.

They come to watch around us here
To soothe our sorrow, calm our fear.
Ye heavenly guides, speed not away
God willeth you with us to stay.

R. Campbell 1814–68

St. Francis of Assisi – October 3rd

A meditation: A saint's way of looking at things

In every work of the artist he praised the Artist; whatever he found in the things made he referred to the Maker. He rejoiced in all the works of the hands of the Lord and saw behind things pleasant to behold their life-giving reason and cause. In beautiful things he saw Beauty itself; all things were to him good.

This is a description of St. Francis, by his biographer, Thomas of Celano, 13th Cent.

A Prayer of St. Francis

You are holy, Lord, the only God,
You do wonders
. . . You are love, charity,
You are wisdom;
You are humility;
You are patience;
You are beauty;
You are meekness;
You are security;
You are inner peace;
You are joy;
You are our hope and joy;
You are justice;
You are moderation
You are all our riches
You are enough for us.

St. Francis of Assisi 1182–1226

St. Luke's Day – October 18th

Matthew, Mark, Luke and John
Bless the bed that I lie on
Four corners to my bed
Four Angels there be spread:
One at the head, one at the feet,
And two to guard me while I sleep.
God within, and God without,
And Jesus Christ all round about;
If any danger come to me,
Sweet Jesus Christ deliver me.
Before I lay me down to sleep
I give my soul to Christ to keep;
And if I die before I wake,
I pray that Christ my soul will take.

A child's evening prayer – Anon.

PRAYERS FOR ALL SAINTS AND ALL SOULS

All Saints – November 1st

Blessed feasts of blessed martyrs
Saintly days of saintly men,
With affection's recollections
Greet we your return again

By contempt of wordly pleasures
And by mighty battles done
Have they merited with angels
To be knit for aye in one.

Wherefore made co-hiers of glory
Ye that sit with Christ on high
Join to ours your supplications
As for grace and peace we cry.

Old German prayer, 12th century

All Saints – November 1st

Blessed are the poor in spirit;
for theirs is the kingdom of Heaven.
Blessed are they that mourn;
for they shall be comforted.
Blessed are the meek;
for they shall inherit the earth.
Blessed are they that hunger and thirst after
righteousness; for they shall be filled.
Blessed are the merciful;
for they shall obtain mercy.
Blessed are the pure in heart;
for they shall see God.
Blessed are the peacemakers;
for they shall be called the children of God.
Blessed are they which are persecuted for
righteousness' sake;
for their is the kingdom of Heaven.
Blessed are ye, when men shall revile you, and
persecute you, and shall say all manner of evil
against you falsely, for my sake.
Rejoice, and be exceeding glad; for so great is your
reward in Heaven; for so persecuted they the
prophets which were before you.

Matthew: 5:3–12

All Souls – November 2nd

'It is a far, far better thing that I do now, than I have ever done; it is a far, far better rest I go to than I have ever known.'

Charles Dickens

That the end of our lives may be Christian, without torment, blameless and peaceful and that we may have a good defence before the fearful Judgement-Seat of Christ, let us entreat. Grant this, O Lord.

From the Divine Liturgy of St. John Chrysostom

All Souls – November 2nd

'Truth it is. I hoped ere this, casting off this body of death, to have kissed the glorified wounds of my sweet Saviour, sitting in the throne of His Father's own glory, which desire hath so quieted my mind that neither the sharpness of death much terrified me nor the shortness of life much troubled me. My sins are great, I confess, but I flee to God's mercy; my negligences are without number, I grant but I appeal to my Redeemer's clememcy. I have no boldness but in His blood; His bitter passion is my only colsolation. It is comfortable that the prophet hath recorded that 'He hath written us in his hands' Oh! that he would vouchsafe to write Himself in our hearts, how joyful would we then appear before the tribunal seat of His Father's glory: the dignity whereof when I think of it, my flesh quaketh, not sustaining, by reason of mortal infirmity, the presence of my Creator's majesty. Our Lord perfect us to that end whereunto we were created, that, leaving this world, we may live in Him and of Him, world without end . . .'

St. Ralph Shervin,
Letter to friends shortly before his martyrdom 1581

All Souls – November 2nd

For as much as it hath pleased Almighty God of His great mercy to take unto Himself the soul of our dear brother here departed, we therefore commit his body to the ground; earth to earth, ashes to ashes, dust to dust; in sure and certain hope of the Resurrection to eternal life, through our Lord Jesus Christ; who shall change our lowly body, that it may be like unto His glorious body, according to the mighty working, whereby He is unable to subdue all things to Himself.

From the Book of Common Prayer.

Lead, kindly light, amid the encircling gloom,
Lead Thou me on,
The night is dark, and I am far from home
Lead Thou me on.
Keep Thou my feet; I do not ask to see
The distant scene; one step enough for me.

John Henry Newman 1801–90

All Souls – November 2nd

Out of the depths have I cried thee, O Lord,
Lord, hear my voice!
Let thine ears be attentive
to the voice of my supplications.

If Thou Lord, shouldst mark iniquities,
O Lord, who shall stand?
But there is forgiveness with thee,
that thou mayest be feared.

My soul waiteth for the Lord,
and in his word do I hope.
My soul waiteth for the Lord
more than they that watch for morning
. . . for daybreak.
Let Israel hope in the Lord, for

with the Lord there is mercy,
and with Him is plenteous redemption.
And he shall redeem Israel
from all his iniquities.

Psalm 130

Remembrance Day – November 11th

War knows no power. Safe shall be my going . . .
Safe though all safety's lost; safe where men fall;
And if these poor limbs die, safest of all.

Rupert Brooke 1887–1915

'They shall grow not old,
as we that are left grow old;
Age shall not weary them, nor the years condemn
At the going down of the sun and in the morning
We will remember them.'

Lawrence Benyon 1869–1943

Remembrance Day – November 11th

'Go forth upon thy journey from this world,
O Christian soul
in the peace of Him in whom thou hast belief
in the name of God the Father, who created thee in
the name of Jesus Christ, who died for thee
in the name of the Holy Spirit,
who strengthened thee.
May angels and archangels,
and all the armies of the heavenly host,
come to meet thee,
may all the saints of God welcome thee,
may thy portion this day be in gladness and peace,
then go forth on thy journey, O Christian soul.

Roman Rite

St. Edmund, King and Martyr – November 20th

O may we tread the sacred road
that saints and holy martyrs trod;
wage to the end the glorious strife
and win, like them, a crown of life.

Rowland Hill 1744–1833 and others

St. Andrew, Patron of Scotland – November 30th

St. Andrew, the Apostle, was a fisherman. His remains are said to have been taken to Scotland and buried there in the place which now bears his name.

This is a famous Scottish grace, to be said before meals, written by Scotland's most famous poet:

The Selkirk Grace

Some hae meat, and canna eat
And some wad eat that want it;
But we hae meat and we can eat
And sae the Lord be thankit.

Robert Burns 1759–96

PRAYERS FOR ADVENT

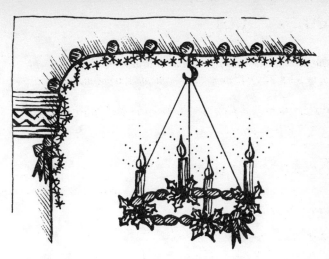

Advent

There is a need for heralds of the Gospel who are
experts in humanity, who have a profound knowledge
of the heart of present-day man, participating in his
joys and hopes anguish and sadness, and who are at
the same time contemporaries in love with God.

Pope John Paul II

O hope of every contrite heart,
O joy of all the meek
To those who fall, how kind Thou art,
How good to those who seek!

But what to those who find? Ah! This
Nor tongue nor pen can show:
The love of Jesus, what it is
None but His lovers know.

11th cent. tr. Edward Caswall 1814–1878

Advent

O come, O come, Emmanuel
And ransom captive Israel
That mourns in lonely exile here
Until the Son of God appear.
Rejoice! Rejoice! Emmanuel
Shall come to thee, O Israel.

Traditional Advent hymn. 18th cent.

Stir up Thy power, we beseach Thee, O Lord, and
come; that from the threatening dangers of our sins
we may deserve to be rescued by Thy protection, and
to be saved by Thy deliverance. Who livest and
reignest with God the Father in the unity of the
Holy Ghost, God, world without end. Amen.

An old Collect for the First Sunday of Advent: traditionally the day on which people 'stir up' their Christmas puddings.

Advent

Saint John the Baptist
who did cry out
to make the roads straight
for the Saviour,
help me and those dear to me
to straighten for Him
the paths of our hearts.

Teach us
by our life
to glorify Him
to confess Him
to love Him.

Help my nation
to understand His teaching,
to proclaim it,
and to live by it. Amen.

Written by four Lithuanian girls, Adele, Lioné, Valé and Levuté in Siberian exile, 1953.

Advent

Jesus, grant me grace to fix my mind on Thee, especially in time of prayer, when I directly converse with Thee. Stop the motions of my wandering head, and the desires of my unstable heart: suppress the power of my spiritual enemies, who endeavour at that time to draw my mind from heavenly thoughts, to many vain imaginations. So shall I, with joy and gratitude, look on Thee as my deliverer from all the evils I have escaped; and as my benefactor for all the good I have ever received, or can hope for... O beloved of my soul, take up all my thoughts here, that mine eyes, abstaining from all vain and hurtful sights, may become worthy to behold Thee face to face in Thy glory for ever.

Richard Whytford, 'The Psalter of Jesus', 16th cent. Whytford, fellow of Queen's College, Cambridge, was a friend of St. Thomas More.

Advent

Hail and blessed be the hour and the moment in which the Son of God was born of the most pure Virgin Mary in a stable at Bethlehem at midnight in the piercing cold. In that hour vouchsafe my God to hear my prayers and grant my desires through the merits of Our Saviour Jesus Christ and of His Blessed Mother. Amen.

A traditional Advent Prayer. It is supposed to be said 15 times a day from 30th November, St. Andrew, to Christmas Day.

Prayer for the Feast of St. Nicholas – December 6th

Heavenly Father, as Christmas draws near we commemorate the feast-day of your beloved Bishop and Saint, Nicholas. We love and honour his memory because of his tender concern for children and for the poor. We thank you for the merriment that his feast has brought down all the centuries. We ask you from the bottom of our hearts to help us to remember, on this his feast-day, that we should try to retain the innocence of childhood and a sincere faith in you all our lives. Show us, too, how to share the good things that we have with others, and to imitate St Nicholas in generosity and goodwill. We ask him to pray for us from his place in Heaven.

Hanukkah, The Jewish Feast of Lights

These candles
which now we light
are in remembrance of the miracle of our
deliverance
of the wondrous and glorious deeds,
that you performed for our fathers of old
and still perform for us today
through your holy priests.
For the eight days of Hanukkah
these candles are holy,
and we cannot look at them
without giving praise and honour you, O Lord,
for the wonders and miracles that you have
performed
and for your glory.

Hymn at the lighting of the candles. Talmud, Sopherim 20,6

Hanukkah commemorates the re-lighting of the perpetual light in the Temple at Jerusalem after the Jews had reconquered it from the Syrians. They had oil for one day but it miraculously lasted 8 days, the time taken to prepare fresh oil. A Hanukkah candle is kept alight for all the 8 days of the feast in a Jewish family.

St. Lucy's Day – December 13th

An old Danish prayer to St Lucy, asking for a good husband.

Sweet St Lucy, let me know
whose cloth I shall lay
whose bed I shall make
whose child I shall bear
whose darling I shall be
whose arms I shall sleep in.

St. Lucy was an early Roman martyr. Her name means 'light' and comes from the same root as lucid, and translucent. The tradition on her day is for the daughter of the family to wear a crown of candles and serve coffee and saffron buns.

PRAYERS FOR CHRISTMAS

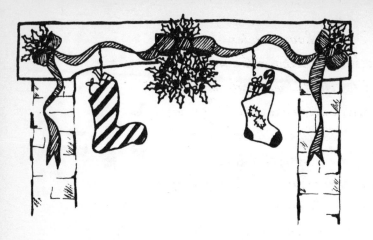

Christmas – December 25th

As I in hoary winter's night
stood shivering in the snow,
Surprised I was with sudden heat,
which made my heart to glow;
And lifting up a fearful eye
to view what fire was near,
A pretty babe all burning bright
did in the air appear;
Who, scorched with excessive heat
such floods of tears did shed,
As though His floods should quench His flames
which with His tears were fed.
'Alas!' quoth He,
'but newly born in fiery heats I fry,
Yet none approach to warm their hearts
or feel my fire but I!'
My faultless breath the furness is;
the fuel wounding thorns;

Christmas – December 25th

Love is the fire, and sighs the smoke,
the ashes and scorns;
The fuel Justice layeth on,
and Mercy blows the coals,
The metal in this furnace wrought
are men's defiled souls;
For which, as now on fire
I am to work to their good,
So will I melt into a bath to wash them in my
blood.'
With this he vanished out of sight
and swiftly shrank away
And straight I called unto mind that it was
Christmas Day.

Robert Southwell 1562–1595

Christmas Day – December 25th

Silent night, holy night
All is calm, all is bright
Round yon virgin Mother and Child
Holy infant so tender and mild.
Sleep in heavenly peace.

Joseph Mohr 1790–1848
tr. John F. Young 1820–85

Christ, the glory of the sky,
Christ, of earth the hope secure,
Only Son of God most high
Offspring of a Maiden pure.

Purest Light, within us dwell,
Never from our souls depart
Come, the shades of each dispel,
Fill and purify the heart.

5th century. tr. R. Campbell 1814–68

God bless us, every one!

Tiny Tim's prayer, from Charles Dickens' 'A Christmas Carol'

Christmas – December 25th

*Little Jesus, wast Thou shy
Once, and just so small as I?
And what did it feel like to be
Out of heaven and just like me?
Didst thou sometimes think of there
And ask where all the angels were?
I should think that I would cry
For my house all made of sky;
And wonder where my angels were;
And at waking 'twould distress me –
Not an angel there to dress me!*

*Hadst Thou ever any toys
Like us little girls and boys?
And didst Thou play in Heaven with all
The angels, that were not too tall,
With stars for marbles? Did the things
Play 'Can you see me?' through their wings?*

Christmas – December 25th

Didst Thou kneel at night to pray,
And didst Thou join Thy hands, this way?
And did they tire sometimes, being young,
And make the prayer seem very long?
And dost Thou like it best, that we
Should join our hands to pray to Thee?
I used to think, before I knew,
The prayer not said unless we do.
And did Thy Mother at the night
Kiss Thee, and fold the clothes in right?
And didst Thou feel quite good in bed,
Kissed, and sweet, and Thy prayers said?

Thou canst not have forgotten all
That it feels like to be small:
And Thou knows't I cannot pray
To Thee in my father's way –
When Thou wast so little, say,
Couldst Thou talk Thy Father's way? –

Christmas – December 25th

So, a little Child, come down
And hear a child's tongue like Thy own;
Take me by the hand and walk,
And listen to my baby-talk.
To Thy Father show my prayer
(He will look, Thou art so fair),
And say: 'O Father, I Thy Son,
Bring the prayer of a little one.'

And He will smile, that children's tongue
Has not changed since Thou wast young!

Francis Thompson 1859–1907

Christmas – December 25th

This little Child
he made all things:
Of Lords the Lord
And King the Kings.

Angels bright they sang that night
And said unto that child:
'Blessed be Thou and so she be
That is both meak and mild'.

15th century

'Mother of Christ, Mother of Christ,
this do I ask of Thee,
the Bliss untold
which thine arms enfold,
the Christ-child upon thy knee.'

Old Hymn – A Christmas Prayer to Mary

Christmas – December 25th

What child is this, who laid to rest
On Mary's lap, is sleeping?
Whom angels greet with anthems sweet
While shepherds watch are keeping?
This, this is Christ the King
Whom shepherds guard and angels sing
Haste, haste to bring Him laud,
the Babe, the Son of Mary.

Why lies he in such mean estate
Where ox and ass are feeding?
Good Christian, fear, for sinners here –
The silent word is pleading;
Nails, spear, shall pierce Him through
The Cross be borne for me, for you
Hail, word made flesh, the Babe,
the Son of Mary.

H. C. Dix

This carol can be sung to 'Greensleeves'

Christmas – December 25th

Our God, Heaven cannot hold Him
Nor earth sustain;
Heaven and earth shall flee away
When he comes to reign
In the bleak mid-winter
A stable-placed sufficed
The Lord God Almighty
Jesus Christ

Christina Rossetti 1830–94

Rejoice rejoice with hart and voyce
In Christes birth this day rejoyce.

Francis Kinwelmershe 1504–80

Feast of St. Stephen
– December 26th

Thank you, Father, for my patron St Stephen, whom I received at baptism. Perhaps I besmirched that name made famous by his martyr's blood? I want to garnish it with my good life and suffering. Give me, Father, the grace to turn heavenward, so that I may know how to pray for my enemies. Saint Stephen, the first martyr, in my life I have brought you little glory, ask the Father of my life to ensure that only glory will flow from my life on to your name, to ensure that Stefan will be a liability no more.

Cardinal Stefan Wyszinski, 1983. Written while under imprisonment by the Communist regime in Poland, 1955.

New Year's Eve

God bless the master of this house
God bless the mistress too
And all the little children
That round the table go.
Love and joy come to you
And to your Wassail too
And God bless you and grant you
A happy New Year.

A Wassail Blessing

New Year's Eve

*Deep peace
of the running wave to you
Deep peace
of the flowing air to you
Deep peace
of the quiet earth to you
Deep peace of the shining stars to you
Deep peace
of the Son of Peace to you.*

An old Celtic blessing